ISBN
Paperback: 979-8-90190-415-2
Hardcover: 979-8-90190-416-9

HOW TO USE THIS RESOURCE

A Quick Guide for Parents & Teachers
It's Cool To Be Smart

What's Included

This resource comes with four powerful tools to support your child's confidence, identity, and love for learning:
- Children's Workbook – Activities for literacy, SEL, and goal-setting
- Teacher Discussion Guide – Questions, prompts, and extension ideas
- Family Worksheet – Simple at-home activities that strengthen family connection and reinforce the book's message

FOR TEACHERS	FOR PARENTS & FAMILIES
1. Read-Aloud Use the book during: - Morning meeting - SEL block - Literacy mini-lessons Pause to ask questions from the Teacher Guide.	1. Read Together Read one page or the whole book. Ask: - "What makes you smart?" - "What did you learn today?"
2. Classroom Discussion Use the guide's: - Before/during/after reading prompts - Vocabulary support - SEL connections - Extension activities	2. Use the Workbook at Home Complete 1–2 pages at a time: - Drawing prompts - Reflection questions - Goal-setting sheets Just 5–10 minutes makes a difference.
3. Workbook Integration Use pages for: - Literacy centers - SEL lessons - Writing time - Small-group reflection	3. Family Worksheet Use the Family Worksheet to: - Start conversations - Build confidence - Celebrate strengths - Create simple learning routines It's designed to be easy, fun, and doable for busy families.
4. Culture & Confidence Building - Create a "Smart Wall" - Use affirmations daily - Celebrate effort and curiosity	4. Create Simple Home Routines Choose one: - 5-minute nightly reading - Affirmations before school - Weekly library visit - Homework check-in

TOGETHER, WE BUILD BRILLIANCE

When parents and teachers send the same message —
"You are smart, capable, and powerful" —
children grow in confidence, identity, and academic pride.

TABLE OF CONTENTS

TEACHER DISCUSSION GUIDE

It's Cool To Be Smart by Mojishola Mason

Grade Levels: PreK–5

Focus Areas: Literacy • SEL • Identity • Academic Confidence

Purpose of This Guide

This guide helps teachers facilitate meaningful conversations before, during, and after reading It's Cool To Be Smart. It supports literacy instruction, SEL competencies, and culturally responsive teaching practices.

Learning Objectives

Students will:

- Build confidence in their academic abilities
- Identify personal strengths and talents
- Engage in meaningful discussion about identity and learning
- Practice comprehension skills (retelling, making connections, identifying themes)
- Demonstrate SEL skills such as self-awareness, self-management, and social awareness

Standards Alignment

Literacy (Common Core–Aligned)

- RL.K–5.1: Ask and answer questions about key details
- RL.K–5.2: Identify central message, lesson, or theme
- RL.K–5.3: Describe characters, settings, and major events
- SL.K–5.1: Participate in collaborative conversations
- L.K–5.6: Use acquired vocabulary to express ideas

SEL (CASEL Framework)

- Self-Awareness: Recognizing strengths, confidence, and positive identity
- Self-Management: Encouraging effort, curiosity, and perseverance
- Social Awareness: Respecting others' abilities and differences
- Relationship Skills: Encouraging supportive peer interactions

Before Reading: Activate Thinking

Use these prompts to set the tone:

- "What does it mean to be smart?"
- "How do you feel when you learn something new?"
- "Why do you think some kids hide their intelligence?"
- "What are some things you're proud of knowing or doing well?"

Optional Mini-Activity:

Students draw or write one thing they are "smart" at — academically or creatively.

During Reading: Pause & Discuss

Choose 2–3 moments to stop and ask:

- "What message do you think the author is trying to share here?"
- "How is the character showing confidence?"
- "What do you notice about the illustrations? How do they make you feel?"
- "Why is it important for kids to see themselves as smart?"

Encourage turn-and-talks to increase student voice.

💬 After Reading: Deep Discussion Questions

Comprehension & Theme

- "What is the main message of the book?"
- "How does the book show that being smart is something to celebrate?"
- "What examples from the story show confidence or pride?"

Identity & SEL

- "What makes you smart?"
- "How can we support each other in being proud of our learning?"
- "Why is it important to see characters who look like you being smart and confident?"

Community & Culture

- "How can our classroom show that it's cool to be smart?"
- "What can we do as a school to celebrate learning?"

✏️ Extension Activities

1. "I Am Smart Because…" Writing Activity

Students complete the sentence:
"I am smart because…"

Then illustrate their response.

2. Smart Goals Wall

Students set one academic goal and post it on a classroom "Smart Goals" board.

3. Identity Shields

Students create shields showing their strengths, talents, and interests.

4. Classroom Mantra

Create a class chant inspired by the book, such as:

"We are smart. We are strong. We are learners. We belong."

5. Family Engagement

Send home a reflection sheet:

- "Ask your child what makes them smart."
- "Share a time when you felt proud of learning something new."

🖼️ Tips for Teachers

- Reinforce the message throughout the year, not just during the read-aloud
- Use the book during SEL blocks, morning meetings, or literacy mini-lessons
- Highlight student strengths publicly and consistently
- Encourage students to celebrate each other's learning

 # STUDENT WORKSHEET PACKET

It's Cool To Be Smart
Literacy • SEL • Identity • Confidence

Worksheet 1: "What Makes Me Smart?"

Directions:

Think about the things you are good at. Draw or write to show what makes you smart.

1. I am smart because I can…

____

____

____

____

2. Draw a picture of yourself being smart.

3. Circle the words that describe you:

- Creative
- Kind
- Hard-working
- Curious
- Brave
- Helpful
- Focused
- A good friend

4. One new thing I want to learn is:

____

____

____

____

____

Worksheet 2: Story Reflection

Directions:

Answer the questions using complete sentences or drawings.

1. What was the main message of the book?

2. How did the book make you feel? Why?

3. What is one part of the story you connected with?

4. Why is it important to be proud of being smart?

Worksheet 3: Vocabulary Builder

Directions:

Match each word to its meaning by drawing a line. Then use one word in a sentence.

Word	Meaning
Brilliant	A strong desire to learn or inquire
Thrive	Responsible for forming long-term memories
Curious	Something bright or intelligent
Hippocampus	To go after something you want
Proud	To grow or develop successfully
Smart	To put pieces together to make something
Dream	To say something clearly and confidently so others know what you believe or decide.
Pursue	A big hope or goal you imagine for your future
Assemble	To learn something so well that you can remember it without looking.
Declare	Able to think, learn, and solve problems well
Memorize	Feeling happy and confident about who you are or something you've accomplished.

Use one word in a sentence:

____

____

____

____

____

Worksheet 4: "My Smart Goals"

Directions:

Set one goal that will help you grow your brain.

My goal is to:

Why this goal is important:

Steps I will take:

1.

2.

3.

How I will celebrate when I reach my goal:

____

____

____

____

____

____

____

____

____

____

Worksheet 5: Text-to-Self Connections

Directions:

Complete each sentence.

1. How I will celebrate when I reach my goal

____

____

____

____

____

2. A time I felt proud of myself was when...

____

____

____

____

____

3. Something I want people to know about me is...

____

____

____

____

____

4. One way I can help others feel smart is...

____

____

____

____

____

Worksheet 6: Identity Shield

Directions:

Draw or write inside each section of the shield.

Sections:

- My Strengths
- My Hobbies
- My Culture
- My Dreams
- What Makes Me Smart

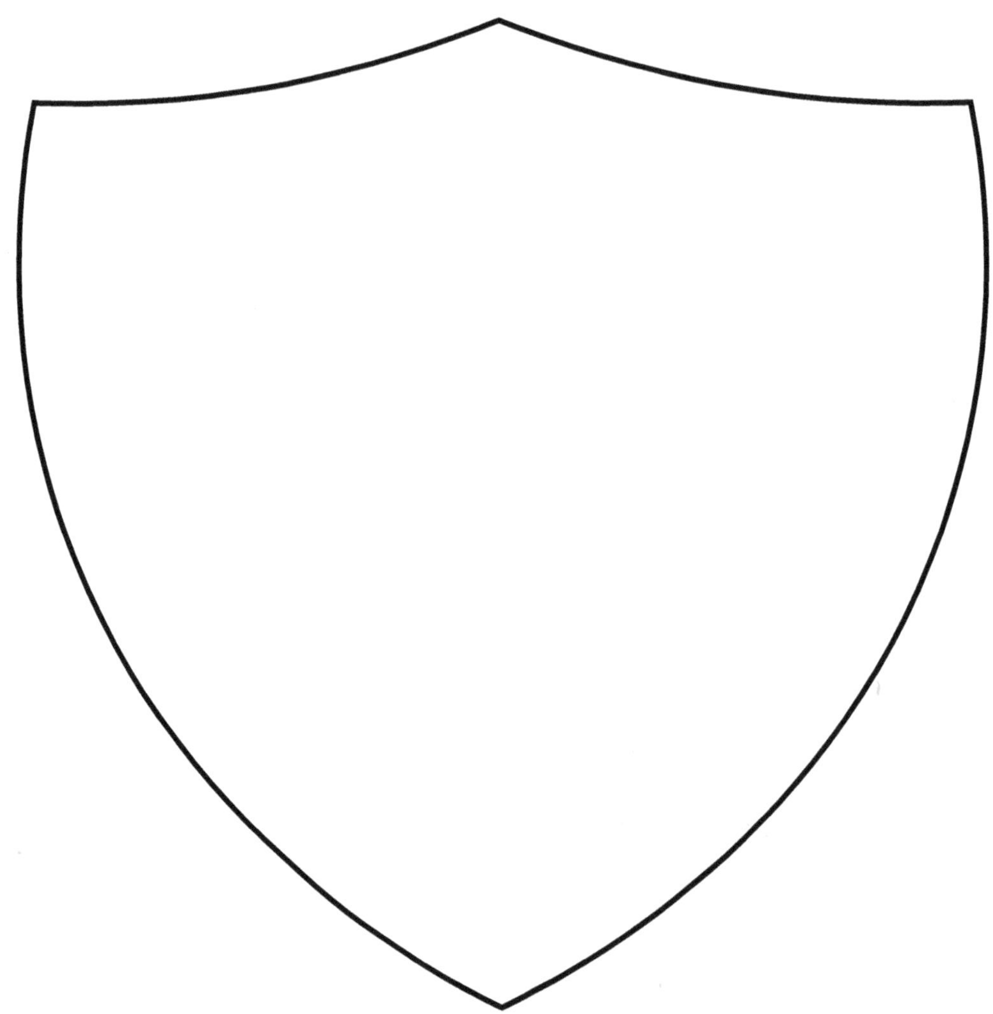

Worksheet 7: "I Can Show I'm Smart By..."

Directions:

Check all that apply, then add your own ideas.

- ○ Asking questions
- ○ Trying my best
- ○ Helping others
- ○ Reading every day
- ○ Staying curious
- ○ Being kind
- ○ Practicing new skills
- ○ Believing in myself

My own ideas:

Worksheet 8: Exit Ticket

Directions:

Complete one sentence

- Today I learned...
- Today I felt proud when...
- One thing I want to remember is...
- I can show I'm smart by...

📘 PARENT ENGAGEMENT CURRICULUM

It's Cool To Be Smart

Strengthening Home–School Partnerships Through Literacy, Identity & Confidence

🌟 PROGRAM OVERVIEW

Directions:

To empower families with tools, language, and activities that reinforce academic pride, positive identity, and a love for learning at home.

Target Audience:

Parents, guardians, caregivers, and family members of students in grades PreK–5.

Program Length:

4–6 sessions (flexible), 45–60 minutes each.

Core Components:

- Literacy engagement
- SEL and identity development
- Family–child bonding activities
- Practical strategies for supporting learning at home
- Community building among families

SESSION OUTLINE (6-Week Model)

SESSION 1 — Welcome & The Power of Identity

Theme: "Every child deserves to feel smart."

Goal:

- Introduce the book and its message
- Build community among families
- Explore how identity and confidence shape learning

Activities:

- Read aloud a short excerpt
- Family reflection: "What makes our child smart?"
- Group discussion: How do we talk about intelligence at home?
- Take-home activity: "Family Smart Shield" (parents + child)

SESSION 2 — Literacy at Home Made Simple

Theme: "Reading is a family superpower."

Goal:

- Teach families easy, low-stress literacy strategies
- Show how to use the children's workbook at home

Activities:

- Model a 5-minute read-aloud routine
- Demonstrate "pause and talk" questions
- Families practice with partners
- Take-home: Bookmark with 5 literacy prompts

SESSION 3 — Building Confidence & Growth Mindset

Theme: "Smart is something you grow."

Goal:

- Help families understand growth mindset
- Provide language to encourage effort, not perfection

Activities:

- "Fixed vs. Growth Mindset" sorting game
- Practice using affirmations
- Create a family mantra
- Take-home: Growth mindset fridge cards

SESSION 4 — Celebrating Culture, Strengths & Brilliance

Theme: "Our culture is part of our intelligence."

Goal:____

- Affirm cultural identity
- Help families connect heritage to learning

Activities:

- "Where We Come From" family map
- Share traditions, languages, strengths
- Discuss how culture shapes confidence
- Take-home: "My Family Story" writing page

SESSION 5 — Helping Children Set Smart Goals

Theme: "Goals help our brilliance grow."

Goal:____

- Teach families how to set simple academic goals
- Use the workbook's goal-setting pages

Activities:

- Model a SMART goal
- Families create a goal with their child
- Share strategies for staying motivated
- Take-home: Goal tracker sheet

SESSION 6 — Family Celebration Night

Theme: "We are a community of brilliance."

Goal:

____

____

____

____

- Celebrate student and family growth
- Strengthen school–family relationships

Activities:

- Student showcase (reading, artwork, identity shields)
- Family photo wall: "It's Cool To Be Smart"
- Certificates of brilliance
- Closing circle: "One thing we're proud of"

💬 KEY MESSAGES FOR FAMILIES

- Every child is smart in many ways
- Intelligence grows with effort and encouragement
- Representation matters — children need to see themselves as brilliant
- Families play a powerful role in building confidence
- Reading together builds connection and academic success
- Culture, identity, and heritage are sources of strength

📈 EXPECTED OUTCOMES

Families will:

- Increase confidence in supporting literacy at home
- Use positive, affirming language about intelligence
- Strengthen relationships with their children
- Build routines that support reading and learning
- Feel more connected to the school community

Students will:

- Show increased confidence and pride
- Engage more in reading and learning
- Strengthen identity and SEL skills
- Feel supported by both home and school

📘 ONE-SESSION PARENT ENGAGEMENT CURRICULUM

It's Cool To Be Smart

Duration: 1 hour 30 minutes

Audience: Parents, caregivers, and children (PreK–5)

Purpose: Strengthen home–school partnership through literacy, identity, and confidence-building activities.

🌟 SESSION TITLE:

Directions: "Celebrating Brilliance: A Family Night with It's Cool To Be Smart"

🕐 SESSION BREAKDOWN (1.5 Hours)

0:00–0:10 — Welcome & Community Warm-Up (10 min)

Goals: Build comfort, connection, and shared purpose.

Activities:

- Greeting families as they arrive

Quick icebreaker:

- "Turn to your child and say one thing you love about how they learn."
- Overview of the session and the message of the book

Key Message:

Every child deserves to feel smart, valued, and confident

0:10–0:25 — Read-Aloud & Identity Discussion (15 min)

Goals: Introduce the book's themes of brilliance, identity, and confidence.

Activities:

- Facilitator reads a short excerpt or selected pages
- Families discuss:
  - "What makes you smart?"
  - "How do we show confidence at home?"

Takeaway:

Children learn best when families affirm their intelligence.

0:25–0:45 — Family Literacy Workshop (20 min)

Goals: Equip families with simple, powerful literacy strategies.

Mini-Lesson:

- How to do a 5-minute read-aloud at home
- How to ask "pause and talk" questions
- How to use the children's workbook for literacy + (Social Emotional Learning) SEL

Hands-On Practice:
Families practice reading a short passage together using the modeled strategies.

Takeaway:
Reading at home doesn't need to be long — just consistent and joyful.

0:45–1:05 — Confidence & Growth Mindset Activity (20 min)

Goals: Strengthen SEL, identity, and academic pride.

Activities:

- "Smart Is Something You Grow" mini-lesson

Families complete the Family Smart Shield together

- Sections include:
    - Our strengths
    - Our culture
    - What makes us smart
    - Our dreams

Families create a Family Mantra, such as:

- **"In this family, we learn, we grow, and we shine."**

Takeaway:
Confidence grows when families celebrate effort, not perfection.

1:05–1:20 — Goal-Setting & Home Learning Plan (15 min)

Goals: Help families set simple, realistic academic goals.

Activities:

- Facilitator models a SMART goal
- Families complete the Goal Tracker together
- Families choose one home routine to support learning (reading time, homework space, affirmation practice)

Takeaway:
Small routines build big confidence.

1:20–1:30 — Celebration & Closing Circle (10 min)

Goals: End with joy, pride, and community connection.

Activities:

- Students share one part of their Smart Shield
- Families share their mantra
- Certificates of Brilliance for each child
- Group photo: "It's Cool To Be Smart" Family Wall

Closing Prompt:
"Say one thing you're proud of about yourself today."

◎ EXPECTED OUTCOMES

Families will leave with:

- A deeper understanding of how to support literacy at home
- Tools to build confidence and identity
- A shared family mantra
- A home learning plan
- A stronger connection to the school community

Students will leave feeling:

- Proud
- Seen
- Confident
- Excited to learn

📘 FAMILY TAKE HOME

It's Cool To Be Smart

A Guide for Families to Build Confidence, Identity & a Love for Learning at Home

🌟 Welcome, Families!

Your child just experienced It's Cool To Be Smart — a joyful, affirming story that celebrates brilliance, confidence, and the power of learning.

This booklet is designed to help you continue that message at home.

Inside, you'll find simple activities, conversation starters, and tools to help your child grow their confidence and celebrate their intelligence every day.

Because in your home… it really is cool to be smart.

📖 1. The Message of the Book

It's Cool To Be Smart teaches children that:

- Intelligence comes in many forms
- Learning is powerful
- Confidence matters
- Culture and identity are strengths
- Every child deserves to feel proud of who they are

As a family, you play a huge role in helping your child believe these truths.

💬 2. Family Discussion Starters

Use these questions during dinner, car rides, or bedtime:

Identity & Confidence

- "What makes you smart in your own way?"
- "What's something you learned today that made you proud?"
- "How does our family show that learning is important?"

Effort & Growth Mindset

- "What was something challenging today, and how did you handle it?"
- "What's one thing you want to get better at?"
- "What can we practice together this week?"

Culture & Brilliance

- "What is something special about our family or culture?"
- "How does our background make us strong and smart?"

3. Easy Literacy Activities for Home

These activities take 5 minutes or less — perfect for busy families.

5-Minute Read-Aloud

- Read one page or one paragraph
- Ask: "What's happening here?"
- Ask: "What does this make you think about?"

Talk About Words

Choose one new word from any book and ask:

- "What do you think it means?"
- "Where else have you heard it?"

Family Writing Moment

Write together for 3 minutes:

- A list
- A sentence
- A memory
- A dream

Audio Learning

- Listen to a short story or podcast and talk about it.

🛡 4. Family Smart Shield Activity

Create a shield that represents your family's brilliance.

Sections to fill in:

- Our Strengths
- Our Culture
- What Makes Us Smart
- Our Dreams
- How We Support Each Other

Prompt:

"Let's draw or write what makes our family strong, smart, and unique."
Hang it on the fridge or a bedroom wall.

💜 5. Family Mantra

Create a simple sentence your family can say every day.

Examples:

- "In this family, we learn, grow, and shine."
- "We are smart, we are strong, we are proud."
- "Our brilliance makes us unstoppable."

Write your own:

____
____
____
____
____
____
____
____

Our Family Mantra:

____
____
____
____
____
____
____
____

◎ 6. Family Goal-Setting Page

Choose one goal to work on together.

Our Goal:____

Why this matters to us:

Steps we will take:

    1.

    2.

    3.

How we will celebrate:

____

____

____

7. Home Learning Routines

Choose one routine to start this week:

- ☐ 5-minute nightly reading
- ☐ Homework space check-in
- ☐ "What did you learn today?" conversation
- ☐ Weekly library visit
- ☐ Affirmation practice ("Say one thing you're proud of")
- ☐ Tech-free family time
- ☐ Family writing night (once a week)

Pick one and stick with it — small routines build big confidence.

# 8. Celebration Page

Use this page to celebrate your child's brilliance.

We are proud of you because:____

Your strengths are: ____

You shine when you: ____

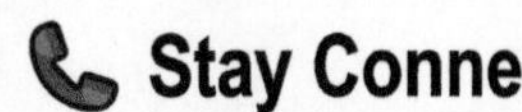 **Stay Connected**

We believe in your child.
We believe in your family.
And we believe that brilliance grows at home.

For school events, author visits, or more resources:

Author: Mojishola Mason

Email: mojisholaa@sholaindustries.com

Facebook: Facebook.com/its cool to be smart

Instagram: @its_cool_to_be_smart

PRE-SURVEY

It's Cool To Be Smart
Student Confidence & Identity Survey (Pre-Reading)
Grades: 2–5 (with optional icons for K–1)

Student Name:___________________________________

Date: _______________________________

1. How do you feel about being smart?
   (Choose one)

   - 😄 I feel very proud

   - 🙂 I feel a little proud

   - 😐 I don't think about it much

   - 🙁 I don't always feel proud

   - 😔 I don't feel smart

2. How confident do you feel in school?

   - ⭐⭐⭐⭐⭐ Very confident

   - ⭐⭐⭐⭐ Confident

   - ⭐⭐⭐ Sometimes confident

   - ⭐⭐ Not very confident

   - ⭐ I rarely feel confident

3. Do you believe you are smart?

   - Yes, definitely

   - Yes, sometimes

   - I'm not sure

   - Not really

   - No

4. What makes you smart?
   (Write or draw)

5. How do you feel when you learn something new?
   - Excited
   - Curious
   - Nervous
   - Frustrated
   - Not sure

6. Do you feel proud of your culture, identity, and who you are?
   - Yes, very proud
   - Mostly proud
   - Sometimes
   - Not really
   - I'm not sure

7. What is one thing you want to get better at this year?

____

____

____

____

 # POST-SURVEY

It's Cool To Be Smart
Student Confidence & Identity Survey (Post-Reading)
Grades: 2–5

Student Name:___________________________________

Date: _______________________________

1. How do you feel about being smart?
   (Choose one)
   - 😊 Very proud
   - 🙂 A little proud
   - 😐 I feel the same as before
   - 🙁 Still unsure
   - 😔 I don't feel smart

2. How confident do you feel in school?
   - ⭐⭐⭐⭐⭐ Very confident
   - ⭐⭐⭐⭐ Confident
   - ⭐⭐⭐ Sometimes confident
   - ⭐⭐ Not very confident
   - ⭐ I rarely feel confident

3. Do you believe you are smart?
   - Yes, definitely
   - Yes, sometimes
   - I'm not sure
   - Not really
   - No

4. What did this book teach you about being smart?

   ____

   ____

   ____

   ____

5. How do you feel about learning new things now?
   - Excited
   - Curious
   - More confident
   - Still nervous
   - Still frustrated

6. Did the book help you feel proud of who you are?
   - Yes, a lot
   - Yes, a little
   - I'm not sure
   - Not really
   - No

7. What is one way you will show you're smart this year?

Optional Teacher Add-On: Growth Reflection

8. What changed for you after reading It's Cool To Be Smart?
   (SEL + identity reflection)

____

____

____

____

____

____

☑ TEACHER ANSWER KEY

It's Cool To Be Smart — Student Worksheet Packet

Worksheet 1: "What Makes Me Smart?" — Answer Key

Purpose: Build confidence, identity, and self-awareness.

Expected Responses:

- Answers will vary widely.
- Look for students identifying strengths such as reading, math, drawing, helping others, being kind, solving problems, or trying their best.
- Drawings should reflect students engaging in something they feel proud of.
- Circled words should reflect how students see themselves — all options are acceptable.
- "One new thing I want to learn" may include academic skills, sports, hobbies, or personal goals.

Teacher Notes:

Affirm every response. The goal is identity-building, not correctness.

Worksheet 2: Story Reflection — Answer Key

1. **Main message of the book:**
   - Being smart is something to celebrate
   - Everyone has strengths
   - Learning is powerful
   - Confidence matters
2. **How the book made them feel:**
   - Expected responses: proud, happy, confident, inspired, excited
   - Encourage students to explain why.
3. **Personal connection:**
   - Students may connect to a character, a feeling, or a moment of pride.
4. **Importance of being proud of being smart:**
   - Helps confidence
   - Encourages effort
   - Shows that learning is valuable
   - Counters teasing or stereotypes

Worksheet 3: Vocabulary Builder — Answer Key

Word	Meaning
Brilliant	Something bright or intelligent
Thrive	To grow or develop successfully
Curious	A strong desire to learn or inquire
Hippocampus	Responsible for forming long-term memories
Proud	Feeling happy and confident about who you are or something you've accomplished.
Smart	Able to think, learn, and solve problems well
Dream	A big hope or goal you imagine for your future
Pursue	To go after something you want
Assemble	To put pieces together to make something
Declare	To say something clearly and confidently so others know what you believe or decide.
Memorize	To learn something so well that you can remember it without looking.

Sentence examples:

- "I have confidence when I try new things."
- "My curiosity helps me learn."
- "My identity includes being a good friend."
- "Reading is one of my strengths."

Worksheet 4: "My Smart Goals" — Answer Key

Purpose: Goal-setting and self-management.

Expected Responses:

- Goals may include reading more, improving math skills, learning a new hobby, or working on behavior/effort.
- Steps should be simple and actionable.
- Celebrations may include sharing with family, telling the teacher, or doing something they enjoy.

Teacher Notes:

Guide students toward realistic, measurable goals.

Worksheet 6: Identity Shield — Answer Key

Sections should include:

- **Strengths:** reading, math, drawing, kindness, teamwork
- **Hobbies:** sports, music, gaming, art, reading
- **Culture:** family traditions, languages, heritage, community
- **Dreams:** future careers, goals, hopes
- **What Makes Me Smart:** effort, curiosity, talents, academic skills

Teacher Notes:

This is a powerful SEL + culturally responsive activity. Encourage students to share.

Worksheet 7: "I Can Show I'm Smart By…" — Answer Key

Expected Responses:

- All checkboxes are valid.
- Student-generated ideas may include:
  - Studying
  - Being creative
  - Asking for help
  - Helping classmates
  - Staying focused
  - Trying again after mistakes

Teacher Notes:

Reinforce that "smart" is about effort, curiosity, and character — not perfection.

Worksheet 8: Exit Ticket — Answer Key

Expected Responses:

- "Today I learned…" → something about themselves, the book, or a skill.
- "Today I felt proud when…" → completing work, sharing, participating.
- "One thing I want to remember…" → the message of the book.
- "I can show I'm smart by…" → effort, kindness, curiosity.

Teacher Notes:

Use responses to guide future SEL and literacy conversations.